ADVENTURE
TO THE
NEW WORLD

BY GRETCHEN MCBRIDE
ILLUSTRATED BY PHYLLIS POLLEMA-CAHILL

Editorial Offices: Glenview, Illinois • Parsippany, New Jersey • New York, New York
Sales Offices: Needham, Massachusetts • Duluth, Georgia • Glenview, Illinois
Coppell, Texas • Ontario, California • Mesa, Arizona

Every effort has been made to secure permission and provide appropriate credit for photographic material. The publisher deeply regrets any omission and pledges to correct errors called to its attention in subsequent editions.

Unless otherwise acknowledged, all photographs are the property of Scott Foresman, a division of Pearson Education.

Photo locators denoted as follows: Top (T), Center (C), Bottom (B), Left (L), Right (R), Background (Bkgd)

Illustrations by Phyllis Pollema-Cahill

ISBN: 0-328-13548-8

Copyright © Pearson Education, Inc.

All Rights Reserved. Printed in the United States of America. This publication is protected by Copyright, and permission should be obtained from the publisher prior to any prohibited reproduction, storage in a retrieval system, or transmission in any form by any means, electronic, mechanical, photocopying, recording, or likewise. For information regarding permission(s), write to: Permissions Department, Scott Foresman, 1900 East Lake Avenue, Glenview, Illinois 60025.

8 9 10 V0G1 14 13 12 11 10 09 08

Author's Note:

    The story you are about to read is a piece of historical fiction. Though based on real events, the dialogue and many details have been invented. We know for a fact that three ships and roughly one hundred English settlers set sail from Portsmouth, England, in April of 1587, bound for the settlement at Roanoke Island in what is now the state of Virginia.

    Among the settlers was a man named John White, who had been appointed governor of Roanoke. White had to sail home to England soon after the group landed, but he promised to return to Roanoke as soon as possible with more supplies and people. However, a war with Spain erupted, delaying White's return.

    Governor White finally returned to Roanoke in the summer of 1590, hoping to find a thriving settlement. Instead, he came across the word CROATOAN, *the name of a Native American tribe, carved into a tree. Other than that puzzling clue, nothing of the settlement remained.*

    To this day, the fate of Roanoke's settlers remains the biggest mystery in the history of England's North American colonies.

Chapter One *Journey's Eve*

It was late April, in the year 1587. Spring had come to the seaport of Portsmouth. For months, Jane's family had been making preparations to leave their life in England behind and start anew in the North American colony of Virginia. Now only a few hours remained until Jane's family and more than one hundred other adventurous English settlers would set sail for the New World.

Jane looked around her small upstairs loft, which she had slept in for as long as she could remember. Her eyes fell upon the yellow curtains that framed the loft's tiny window. She touched them, sending them gently rustling. Jane was pleased with the way the sun shone through the curtains. It bathed the room in a golden glow.

As the evening light faded, Jane tried to imagine leaving her wonderful little loft, her friends and relatives, and everything else that was familiar to her in Portsmouth. She thought of the voyage tomorrow and what life would be like at Roanoke, the island on the coast of the Virginia colony that was the settlers' destination. What did the future hold in store for them?

Jane's mother stood at the top of the stairway, watching with a smile as her daughter daydreamed.

"Dear, you need to do your packing tonight for the voyage," she said, speaking quietly. "The ship leaves early, with the morning tide. Your father is having the trunks brought down to the wharf immediately after breakfast. Remember to bring only things that we need—clothes and not much else. I've packed blankets, food, and medicine."

Jane nodded. "Don't worry; I'll have my packing finished before sunset. But I'm scared about journeying to the New World. How do we know that it will be safe for us there? How do we know that we will get there without any problems? I have so many worries. Are you sure that we must go?"

"Yes, dear, I'm afraid we must," Jane's mother gently explained. "Your father and I have already talked about this. Our space on the ship is already reserved, and we have settled all our business here in Portsmouth. We can't turn back now."

Jane's mother saw that her daughter was frightened and tried to reassure her. "I know how hard it is for you, Jane. I'm finding it as difficult to say goodbye as you are. It won't be easy for us to leave behind the comforts of civilization for an unknown land that promises challenges and hardships."

She went on, "But the opportunities in Virginia are enormous. Queen Elizabeth's plan to settle this Virginia colony and make it grow is positively inspired. Right now it may seem like we are fleeing Portsmouth for an uncertain future. But I assure you, Jane, we'll be the envy of England when they hear of how well we are doing in the New World. Soon all of our friends and relatives will want to join us!"

"I'm sure you're right, Mother," Jane said. "I promise I'll do my best not to grow sad. From now on, I'll think only of the happy future that awaits us in Virginia!"

"Good," her mother replied. "Now make sure to tuck yourself into bed as soon as you're done packing. You need to get a good night's sleep. Tomorrow will be a long day."

Jane's mother started down the stairs. "Good night, Jane," she called out, the sound of her footsteps echoing behind her.

"Good night, Mother," Jane answered. As soon as her mother left, Jane finished selecting the things that she would need for the voyage and for Roanoke. Paying heed to her mother's advice, she gathered only the most essential items–candles, clothing, scissors, and her small loom and sewing kit. Jane took one last look around her loft, then blew out the candle and climbed into bed.

Jane dreamt that night that she had been brought before Queen Elizabeth at the English royal court. Wearing her finest clothing, she stood before the Queen and the royal advisors. The Queen glittered in her crown and jewelry. Her advisors, serious and formal in their official uniforms, scowled and looked menacing. Jane was explaining to the Queen that she would do everything she could to make Roanoke a successful colony, but the advisors were shaking their heads and whispering in the Queen's ear. Jane was about to plead with the advisors when the sunrise burst into her room, waking her from her dream.

Chapter Two *Setting Sail*

"Jane, wake up!" her mother called from downstairs. The morning was chilly. Jane dressed in her wool stockings, skirt, and cloak, bundled up her things for the voyage, and raced down to the first floor. There she found her father sitting at the small table next to the fireplace, packing and checking the trunks while Jane's mother cooked.

"Good morning, Jane. Ready for our voyage to Virginia?" he called out cheerfully.

"As ready as I'll ever be," Jane answered. "Here are my things for the trip. Is there anything you need me to do?"

"Nothing, other than eat!" her father answered. "Your mother has some porridge ready. Once we're done eating, your mother and I will check the house one more time. Then I'll have the trunks taken to the wharf, and we'll walk down to our ship!"

"But what happens to the house, father?" Jane asked.

"Well, the landlord said that the new tenants will arrive as soon as we leave. So it's no longer ours. But you know what? In Virginia, we won't have to rent anymore. There, we'll be able to build a house for ourselves, and we'll have plenty of land on which to grow our crops. No more dirty, cold, crowded Portsmouth!"

"I'll eat to that!" Jane responded, feeling her father's excitement.

Jane and her family finished eating. Jane's father paid some laborers to move the trunks, and the family walked down to the wharf, giving one final glance to their home.

The scene at the wharf was chaotic. People were shouting, laughing, bumping into each other, and bustling about in frantic preparation. A sense of excitement filled the air as everyone thought ahead to the ocean crossing and the new lives that they would make for themselves in the Virginia colony.

The ship's sailors called for everyone to step on board, and Jane's family pushed their way on, jostling for space with the other passengers. One of the sailors was helping passengers place their trunks deep in the ship's hold. As Jane's parents worked with the sailor to move their trunks, Jane stared up at the complex web of spars, lines, and masts that made up the ship's rigging. *It's all so complicated*, she thought to herself. *How does it make the ship sail?*

Jane continued to watch, fascinated, as the sailors scrambled across the decks and prepared the ship. After several moments of intense work, they cast off from the wharf, and raised the sails. The ship plunged forward in the morning breeze. They were off!

Jane waved to the crowd of friends and relatives that had gathered at the end of the wharf to say goodbye. As their ship moved out of the harbor, Jane noticed that there were two other ships traveling with them.

The next couple of days went by slowly as the ships struggled to claw their way west. It was difficult sailing, for they had to fight against the winds and waves that funneled through the narrow English Channel. Jane felt sorry for the sailors, who had to constantly scramble up and down the ship's rigging in order to take down and put up sails. It looked like a hard life!

At last, after stopping briefly at the port of Plymouth to take on more supplies, the ships broke out into the open waters of the Atlantic, just past the westernmost edge of the English coast. Immediately they turned south, to catch the trade winds that would take them into milder weather and warmer water. A full three months of sailing lay ahead.

Chapter Three *Across the Atlantic*

While the fleet was at sea, there was little for the passengers to do other than think of the future. They knew that they would face unknown dangers in the New World. Jane and her family took heart, however, in stories that the sailors told them about previous voyages of exploration along the Virginia coast. The sailors spoke of a country where the winters were short and mild and the summers were warm and comfortable. From what they had seen of the lush forests, many rivers, and green fields, it looked as if the land in the New World could grow anything. For a group of settlers that knew little about what lay ahead of them, such stories were reassuring. Jane listened to the sailors talk and dreamed of a pleasant life at Roanoke.

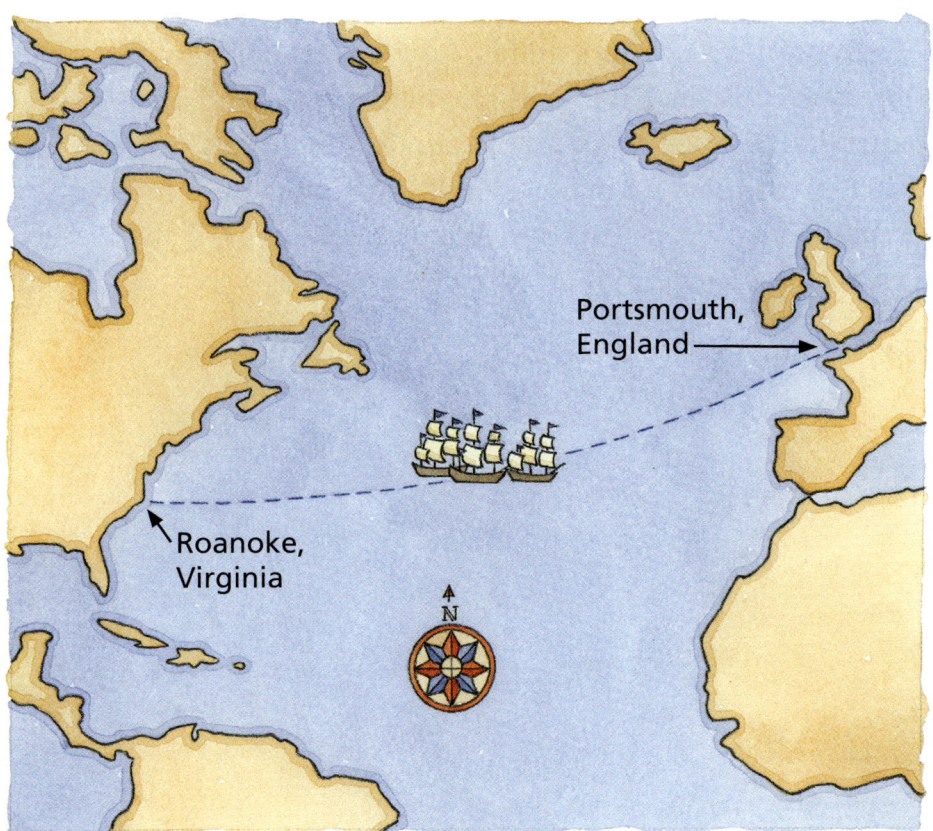

Jane and the other passengers also took comfort from the fact that they would be greeted by a small group of English soldiers when they arrived at Roanoke. During the previous year, a large group of colonists had left Roanoke and returned to England after running low on supplies and encountering difficulties with the local Indians. The leaders of Roanoke wouldn't allow the island to be totally abandoned, so they had a dozen soldiers sent over from England to guard the settlement until Jane's family and everyone else arrived.

There was other good news as well. The soldiers at Roanoke had built a strong fort from the towering oak trees that grew all over the island. Jane and her family hoped that the soldiers had kept the fort in good repair, since they would have to depend upon it for shelter and safety until they built their own houses. The issue of safety preyed on the settler's minds, now that they knew that the previous colonists had had trouble with the Indians of the area. Jane herself was curious about the Indians. She felt sure that she could make friends with them and improve relations between the English and the Indians, if she were given the chance.

The months at sea passed. One day Jane's father took her up on deck to see if they could spot land. As they gazed, he talked about the history of the English colonies.

"The story of our colonies is the story of a friendship," Jane's father explained. "For years, Queen Elizabeth and the great Sir Walter Raleigh have been close friends. A few years ago, they met to form a strategy for England's future. They knew that Spain, our greatest enemy, had grown rich off of her colonies, and were convinced that she would someday use those riches to try and defeat us. So Raleigh and the Queen decided to start planting colonies of our own. Hopefully, they will provide the resources we need to help us defeat Spain!"

A worried look crept across Jane's face. Her father reassured her, "Oh, don't worry, Jane. The Spanish won't threaten us in Roanoke. Their colonies are way to the south and Roanoke has no value to them. But it is very valuable to us, being our first colony in the New World!"

At that moment, the ship's lookout sang out "Land Ho! It's Roanoke!" Everyone gave a shout of joy. They had made it! The little fleet's captains had been able to steer the ships directly to Roanoke, without being blown off course by currents or bad weather.

Chapter Four *Is This Roanoke?*

It was now July 22. Roanoke had been sighted late in the afternoon, so the captain of Jane's ship decided to anchor right off the beach for the evening. Throughout the night, Jane, her family, and the other colonists busied themselves with preparations for stepping onshore in the morning. After three months at sea, the passengers were tired. But they were eager to see Roanoke for the first time, and to greet the other English settlers.

Jane's family and the other settlers rowed ashore the following morning, landing on a white, sandy beach. Among them was a man named John White, who had been appointed Governor of Roanoke. White guided them up from the beach and through a dense forest to a small clearing where Roanoke's fort and settlement lay.

However, when they got there, they were greeted by a nasty shock.

There was almost nothing left of the original settlement! The fort which had promised the settlers shelter and safety had been burned to the ground. Scattered about were a few log houses that had obviously been abandoned long since. Deer grazed around the forest's edge, quite unconcerned by the sudden appearance of Governor White and the other colonists. Other than the sound of a passing breeze, there was only silence.

The colonists turned to face Governor White, looking afraid and concerned. Jane's father spoke up first, his voice loud and demanding.

"I don't understand, Governor White. We were told that there would be soldiers and a fort here. The soldiers have vanished and the fort is ruined. What has happened here?"

Governor White looked around uneasily, trying to come up with an answer that would satisfy both the settlers and himself. But all he could do was shrug his shoulders.

"I don't know," he admitted. "Perhaps they ran into trouble with the Indians. Or maybe they had to move away in order to find food and water. But all is not lost. If we get to work now on building shelters and planting crops, then there's a good chance we'll survive the winter. The harder we work to rebuild this colony, the safer we will be!"

Chapter Five Rebuilding

Inspired by Governor White's passionate speech, the colonists began work that day to rebuild the Roanoke settlement. The men took some axes into the forests to cut down trees. Using chisels, hammers, and nails, they assembled the logs into a frame for the new fort. Then they patched up the gaps between the logs with tree sap. For a roof, the women pulled up tall grasses from a nearby field and wove them together into a tight mesh.

Several days later, the settlers completed the fort. The fort still needed much work, and it became terribly hot at night with everyone packed inside it to sleep. But at least it provided a temporary shelter. Each settler family soon built their own shelter, making the situation at the fort far more bearable. Within a couple of weeks the settlement was dotted with tiny but neat little houses. Then the real work began.

The next task was to get some crops planted before the planting season ended. The men began by chopping down swaths of trees to make clearings. They then built wooden plows and hitched them to horses that they had brought over on the ship. Taking turns with the horses, they furrowed acre after acre of land.

The women followed behind the men, casting onto the furrowed fields the seeds of wheat and other grains that they had brought with them from England. The seeds, nourished by Virginia's warm rain, grew rapidly, promising a healthy harvest.

While waiting for the harvest to ripen, the settlers lived off of the domestic animals they had brought along. From the pigs they made ham and bacon, from the goats they drew milk, from the sheep they spun wool for clothing, and from the chickens they gathered eggs.

The settlers also took advantage of the forest's bounty, gathering walnuts and chestnuts from the vast woods that surrounded Roanoke. When there was time they went hunting for deer, using the guns they had brought from England. When they were lucky they would come back with enough meat to throw a feast for the entire settlement!

Chapter Six *What About the Indians?*

One night in mid-August, while eating dinner with her family, Jane realized how much her family had accomplished in Roanoke. Her father, using an ax, chisel, hammer, and nails, had built tables and chairs. Jane and her mother, using pig's fat, had made tallow candles. From sheep's wool they had woven rugs, blankets, and coverings for the doors and windows. Everything they had, they had made with their own hands!

As they sat eating, the family's thoughts turned from the frantic work of the past weeks towards larger concerns. Jane brought up the mystery of the previous settlers' fate.

"Is it possible that they left because of bad weather, such as a storm?" she asked.

Jane's father frowned, then answered, "A storm like a hurricane certainly might have threatened the houses. But if that was the case, then what happened to the fort? No, it couldn't have been a storm. Clearly it was a fire that destroyed the fort and caused the soldiers to abandon the settlement entirely. But who set it? And for what reason?"

The family thought in silence until Jane, seeing the serious expressions on her parents' faces as they thought about the previous settlers' fates, changed the subject. "One day, while I was playing outside the fort with the other girls, I heard Governor White talking with some of the men about needing to 'establish relations' with the nearby Indians. Everyone says they're bound to cause us trouble. What are they really like?"

Jane's father sighed. "Nobody really knows anything about the Indians. There has been talk that the soldiers may have mistreated them, and because of that the Indians might have fought back. On the other hand, some people say that the Indians might have been so nice to the soldiers that the soldiers decided to go live among them!"

"Oh, my," Jane's mother exclaimed, putting down her fork. "Would English people really do that?"

"They just might have," said Jane's father. "For one thing, as strange and different as these Indians are, there are rumors that they live better than we do. I've heard stories from some of the men who have stumbled onto one of their villages. They said that the Indian's houses were better built than ours. They also said that they have more animal skins drying out in the sun. That means they're better hunters. Also, the Indians' crops were growing much higher than ours. So they're also better farmers, I suppose."

"You really think they're better than we are?" Jane asked.

"It's not that they're better than we are," her father replied. "After all, we have many things—guns, iron tools, and glass—that they don't have. But our ignorance of this land has caused us to make many blunders."

Jane's father then ticked off a list of failures that the settlers had experienced because of their lack of knowledge. "We tried growing crops from seeds we brought from England, only to learn that some of those crops only grow back home. We tried using certain trees to build houses, only to find out that the timber here can't be used in the same way as the timber back in England. We tried eating some of the nuts and berries of the forest, only to find out that some of them make people sick. It's all right, though, because we're learning. We're learning, and we're adapting."

Chapter Seven *Jane Makes a Decision*

Jane was bored by all of her father's talk. In fact, when she thought about it, she was pretty much bored with everything. It seemed as if all she ever did anymore was help weed the garden with her mother, thatch the roof with her father, and tend to any number of the dozens of daily chores that needed to be done. Her frustration with life at Roanoke came bursting out all of a sudden.

"So what if we're learning and adapting? It's still taking too long!" she said defiantly. "I'm curious about these Indians. I want to know what they know. Maybe there are Indian girls my age that I could play with. This village of theirs sounds interesting, and I'm going to go find it!"

Jane's father looked at her sternly. "Jane, you are not allowed to talk to us that way," he said in a very serious voice. "I know that you miss your friends at home and that there aren't as many children to play with here. But we still don't know what happened to the soldiers who were guarding the fort. We don't know if what happened to them involves the nearby Indians, and no one is allowed to visit the Indians unless they have permission from Governor White. You will *not* go looking for their village!"

"Hmmph," Jane replied, getting up from the table. Upset by her father's order but not wanting to anger him any further, she marched off to sleep on her simple straw bed.

Jane woke up early the next day. As she lay in bed, she could hear her parents in their bed, talking about the settlement's problems. The people of Roanoke were under a lot of stress. The Queen and her advisors had demanded that Governor White find a way to make the colony profitable. Powerful people in England had spent large amounts of money to outfit the settlers' ships for the voyage across the Atlantic, and those investors wanted a return on their investment.

The people back home were especially anxious to make money because of the previous failures to make Roanoke work. Jane's parents and other settlers knew that the Queen and her advisors would be angry with them if they failed to grow abundant crops and find gold and silver. But the settlers knew that the only way they could grow better crops and find gold and silver was if they asked the Indians for advice!

Jane heard her father say, "I don't care what the Queen's advisors are demanding from us. The Indians are many and we are few. Until they send more soldiers and weapons, it is foolish for us to seek contact with the Indians."

Jane had had enough. *The adults are frightened for no reason!* she thought. Although Jane had never told her parents about the incident, she remembered the time when she had come across the Indian village while out in the woods picking berries. Jane had been too afraid to do anything other than peek at the village from behind a thick growth of trees. Still, she knew how to get back to it. Jane decided that she would sneak out to meet one of the Indians. She would prove that they were friendly!

As quietly as she could, Jane put on her clothes and snuck out of the house. She tiptoed her way to the edge of the forest and picked up the main hunting trail, only to veer off after a couple hundred yards. Passing a stream, Jane crept towards a small clearing. There she could see some scattered campfires, a small plot of corn, and . . .

Chapter Eight *The Encounter*

. . . *Smack!* Right at that moment, Jane bumped into a young Indian girl. The force of the blow left them momentarily stunned. Rubbing their foreheads in pain, they looked up to see what they had run into.

It was the opportunity that Jane had been waiting for. At last she would be able to find out about these Indians! Summoning her courage, she stammered, "H-h . . . hello."

The native girl, still wincing in pain, looked at Jane directly but did not speak. She looked terrified.

"Hello," Jane tried again, this time with a smile.

"Hello," repeated the native girl.

"You speak English!" Jane exclaimed in wonder.

The native girl again said, "Hello." This time, however, she met Jane's smile with one of her own.

"I was just out for a walk. I have been wanting to meet your people for some time," Jane explained. "Would you show me back to your village?"

The Indian girl had a confused look on her face.

Jane, not understanding that the Indian girl (who in truth knew not a word of English) was only mimicking her, said, "Perhaps you don't speak English as I do. But you still knew the word 'hello,' so you must have known some English people. Oh, I must tell my parents and Governor White!"

The Indian girl still looked confused. But her look quickly changed, as if she had suddenly had an idea. She pointed to a spot deep into the woods, grabbed Jane's hand, and broke into a brisk walk.

I guess she wants to show me something. I better follow! Jane thought, having no idea where she was being led.

The Indian girl led Jane along a faint, densely overgrown path. Jane could still see the clearing where the Indian village lay. But their current path was taking them far from where they had met.

They stopped in a small grove of bushes. Taking Jane's hand for a moment, the Indian girl made Jane pluck one of the ripe red fruits from one of the bushes. It was a juicy, fresh raspberry!

The Indian girl made a motion for Jane to eat the raspberry, while she herself plucked a few more. Jane hesitated. She knew about raspberries but had never eaten one. Back in Portsmouth they had been too expensive for her family to buy. Jane then saw the Indian girl eat one of the raspberries. Relaxing a bit, Jane took a bite. It was delicious!

Jane and the Indian girl stood for several moments, smiling and eating raspberries. Then the Indian girl motioned with her hand, pointing to herself and then the Indian village that lay beyond the edge of the woods. She pointed to Jane and seemed to be inviting her to visit the Indian village.

From out of the corner of her eye, Jane saw the sun climbing steadily above the treetops. She realized that she had been gone for hours. "It's getting late!" Jane exclaimed in a panicked voice. "I must go."

Before Jane left, the Indian girl plucked a handful of raspberries and placed them in Jane's hand.

"Thank you, these are wonderful!" Jane said. "I will come back and visit you soon." She took the Indian girl's hand and shook it. The sudden gesture startled the girl, and at first she didn't know what to do. But then she smiled and shook back. They had become friends. With one last gesture Jane waved good-bye and raced back home.

Chapter Nine *A Time of Uncertainty*

As soon as Jane stepped inside her house, she knew she was in trouble. Her father grabbed her arm and demanded to know where she had been.

Jane sucked in her breath. In a low, sobbing voice, she said, "Oh, Father, I know you and Mother are upset with me. But I had to go see for myself what these Indians were like. This morning I snuck off to a place in the woods where I know an Indian village is. There I met a nice Indian girl–and look, she gave me these delicious raspberries. See, Father, we just might be able to become friends with these Indians!"

Jane's father relaxed his grip on her arm. "You're right, Jane–I am upset with you," he said. "I am upset with you for your foolish venture to the far edge of the settlement. And I am especially upset because you disobeyed my order. I told you that you are not allowed to go beyond our village!"

Jane looked as if she was about to cry. Sighing, her father gave her a hug, saying, "And yet here you are, back safe and sound. Still, you must be punished for your reckless actions. Every night for a month, you are to go to bed immediately after dinner. When you wake up in the morning, you will come to Mother and me before doing anything else. That way we'll know that you're safe. But I do forgive you, Jane. And I'm glad you're home!"

Just at that moment, Governor White came through the front door, followed by a group of men. Stopping at the sight of Jane, he threw his hands in the air.

"So the girl is safe and sound at home!" Governor White exclaimed. He looked down to address Jane. "Well, Jane, you've certainly given the people of Roanoke a fright. Your father and mother approached me this morning at the fort. They were frantic with worry, saying that you had disappeared into the woods. They told me how curious you were about Indians. They thought you might try to run away and join them!"

Governor White turned to face the group of men. "Well, as you can see gentlemen, the girl is safe. Thank you for helping to search for her. You may now return to your homes," he said, dismissing them with a wave of his arm.

In a firm but kindly voice, Governor White said, "Jane, I must say that I'm disappointed with you. You disobeyed your parents and forced us to draft a dozen men to go looking for you. Your little escapade has cost our settlement both time and money. And yet . . ." here his tone softened, ". . . and yet we are at a critical juncture with these Indians. Soon I will go conduct peace talks with them. In order to be successful I need all the information I can get regarding these strange and mysterious people. So tell me, Jane, what did you see?"

Jane hesitated. Should she tell him everything? At last, she settled on telling the truth. "I met an Indian girl. She was about my age. The girl said 'hello' when I talked with her, but other than that said nothing. She took me to a place where some raspberries were growing, and we ate some of them together. Then she seemed to be inviting me to her village, but I knew I had to get back home."

Governor White was satisfied that Jane had told the truth. Still, he could not hide the disappointment in his voice. "Well, if that's all that happened, then we'll have to be content with that. I wish the Indian girl had taken you to her village so you could have learned something of how her people live, but that would have been dangerous. On the other hand, hearing that you had a friendly encounter with an Indian gives me hope for the future. Perhaps there's yet a chance that we will be able to live in peace with these people."

Governor White turned to leave the house. Pausing at the door, he addressed the family. "Before I return to the fort for my official duties, I must remind you all that we live in a time of uncertainty. There is still a chance that this settlement might not survive. We've done well enough through the summer. The crops that we have planted should last through much of the winter. But it might not be enough. Our hunting parties have had success of late, but I don't know if the meat that they've brought in will be enough to make up the difference before spring arrives and English ships can resupply us."

He continued, "Unfortunately, I will not be able to serve Roanoke much longer, for I have been called back by the Queen. My ship sails next week for England. When I return to our mother country, I will ask for the extra goods and supplies that we need to ensure that Roanoke can live on as a permanent settlement. However, it takes three months to sail across the ocean and another three months to sail back. And that doesn't include the time it will take me to plead our settlement's cause before the Queen and her advisors. So the earliest I will be back is next summer. In the meantime, I am proud of everything that we have accomplished here. This colony has adapted well to the challenges of the New World. So good-bye for now, and good luck."

No one spoke for several moments after Governor White left the house. Finally, Jane asked her father anxiously, "Are Governor White's words really true? Do you think this colony is failing? If it fails, does that mean we have to sail back to Portsmouth? What will happen?"

Her father shrugged, saying, "Neither I nor your mother can predict what will happen. I hate having to say so, but Governor White's words are true, Jane. There's still a strong chance that this colony will fail. This first winter will be our strongest test. But while it's still summer and the weather is warm, we might as well do everything we can to try and make Roanoke succeed. By next year, we should be able to have a successful crop. Let's go out to your mother's garden and see how our plants are doing."

The family went out into the garden. Nobody said a word. Although they were frightened by Governor White's words, they had confidence in their ability to survive through the winter and make Roanoke a success. Jane's family faced an uncertain future. But they refused to give up.

Roanoke: The Lost Colony

So what happened to the vanished settlers of Roanoke? Some think they joined the Croatoan Indians, who lived near Roanoke on what is now called Hatteras Island. In 1997, archaeologists unearthed copper and brass pieces and parts of lead bullets from the remains of Hatteras Island's main Croatoan village. Then, in 1998, archaeologists digging at the same site found a gold ring, the kind worn by sixteenth-century English noblemen.

In combination with the CROATOAN carving found at Roanoke in 1590 by John White, these discoveries support the theory that there may have been English people living among the Croatoans during the late sixteenth century. But until archaeologists find evidence that proves beyond a doubt what happened to the Roanoke settlers, we can only make educated guesses as to their fate.